D1397195

# OUR WORLD IN COLOR
# PORTUGAL

OUR
WORLD IN
COLOR

# PORTUGAL

Photography by Steve Vidler
Text and captions by Julia Wilkinson

The Guidebook Company Limited

Copyright © 1991 The Guidebook Company Limited,
Hong Kong

All rights reserved, no part of this publication may be reproduced
or transmitted in any form or by any means, electronic or
mechanical, including photocopy, recording or any information
storage and retrieval system, without permission from
the publisher.

Distributors

**Australia and New Zealand:** The Book Company,
100 Old Pittwater Road, Brookvale, NSW 2100, Australia.

**Canada:** Prentice Hall Canada,
1870 Birchmount Road, Scarborough, Ontario MIP 257, Canada.

**Hong Kong:** China Guides Distribution Services Ltd.,
14 Ground Floor, Lower Kai Yuen Lane, North Point, Hong Kong.

**India and Nepal:** UBS Publishers' Distributors Ltd.,
5 Ansari Road, Post Box 7015, New Delhi 110 002, India.

**Singapore and Malaysia:** MPH Distributors (S) PTE Ltd.,
601 Sims Drive, No. 03/07-21, Pan-I Complex, Singapore 1438.

**USA:** Publishers Group West Inc.,
4065 Hollis, Emeryville, CA 94608, USA.

Photography by Steve Vidler
Text by Julia Wilkinson
Edited by Nick Wallwork
Designed by John Ka Wa Ng

Printed in China

ISBN 962-217-116-8

Right
*The Torre de Belém is the
most striking symbol of
Portugal's Golden Age, a
delightful Manueline tower
with Moorish trimmings.
Built in the early 1500s,
during the last years of
King Manuel's reign, it was
originally surrounded by
the waters of the Tagus
River and guarded the
entrance to the port.*

Following Pages: (Pages 6-7)
*Perhaps the prettiest
walled town in Portugal,
Obidos has enchanted
visitors for over 700 years:
in 1228 King Dinis gave it
to his new wife as a
present, establishing a
royal tradition that lasted
until 1833. Part of the
fortified castle at the
northern end has been
transformed into a
pousada.*

Pages 8-9
*The Algarve's 270km (167
mile) coastline has
everything from sandy
beaches and salt lagoons to
rugged clifftops and rocky
coves. The most dramatic
stretch is this area around
the Ponta da Piedade near
Lagos, with its many
grottoes and rocky
outcrops.*

Pages 10 & 11
*Dozens of carnivals, fairs
and religious festivals or
romarias (held in honour
of a patron saint), are held
in Portugal throughout the
year, especially during the
summer, in the northern
Costa Verde region. Here,
the Portuguese like nothing
better than the chance to
sing and dance and dress
up in their traditional
finery.*

Pages 12-13
*Dreaming beside the
willowy Tãmega River, the
lovely town of Amarante
hosts a thinly-disguised
fertility festival every June
at the Feast of São
Gonçalo, the patron saint
of marriages. The saint's
effigy (his face worn away
by devotees' kisses) lies in
the huge convent which
dominates the town.*

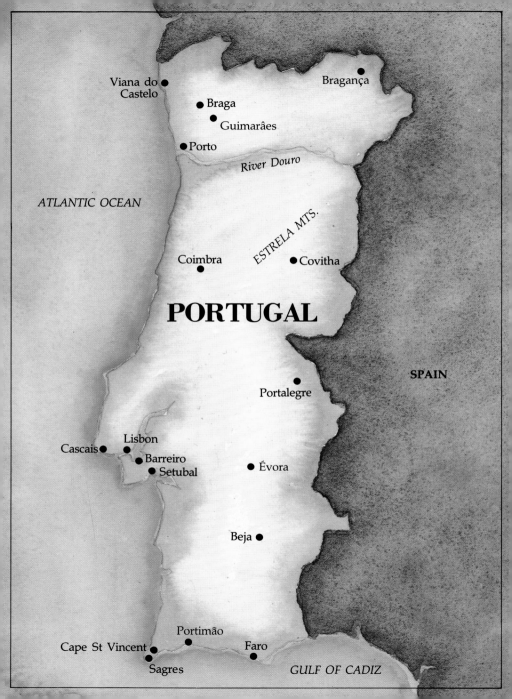

# INTRODUCTION

**P**ERCHED at the end of the Iberian Peninsula, in the westernmost corner of Europe, Portugal has always been a land apart, on the fringe, lining the forgotten hem of Europe. No insurmountable barriers separate it from Spain. Only a strip of water keeps Africa away. You'd have thought it would have been snapped up long ago, a tasty morsel for the Moors of Morocco or the Kings of Castile.

It almost was. But Portugal is a plucky little place. It established its frontiers as long ago as the thirteenth century—which makes it one of the oldest countries in Europe. The very earliest historical evidence shows a determination to keep invaders at bay. And a later independent spirit was to turn this tiny country, not much bigger than Austria or the state of Indiana, away from Europe entirely and out into the unknown world, changing the course of history with its discovery of the sea route to India.

'This is the story of heroes who, leaving their native Portugal behind them, opened a way to Ceylon, and further, across seas no man had ever sailed before,' begins Luis de Camoes in his sixteenth century epic on the Great Discoveries.

'They were men of no ordinary stature, equally at home in war and in dangers of every kind: they founded a new kingdom among distant peoples, and made it great.'

The Portuguese empire spread over five continents, from Macau to Mozambique, Goa to Brazil. In its brief heyday it was the richest and most powerful country in the world—or certainly of half the world.

For Portugal had once ranked with Spain as one of Europe's Christian superpowers. In 1494, with the Pope's blessing, they had signed an extraordinary treaty and by spinning a globe, and drawing a line, had simply divided the world between them. Exquisite cathedrals from that time still stand as showpieces throughout the land, brimming with confidence, entwined with motifs of the sea.

It couldn't last, of course. And somehow, in the process of losing its empire, Portugal also lost its allure. Even as recently as this century, Evelyn Waugh shared most people's views when he wrote of Lisbon, 'There is no European capital of antiquity about which one hears so little.'

Portugal became again the land on the edge, escaping by the skin of its teeth from being swallowed up by Spain and conquered by Napoleon, but escaping attention, too: always that little bit too far to be included in the European Grand Tour or too often wracked with political turmoil. After 1910, the year the monarchy was overthrown and Portugal became a republic, there were 45 changes of government within 16 years, followed by 40 repressive years of dictatorship, and a failed left-wing revolution.

Only slowly, since 1976, has Portugal started to emerge from the shadows, to tug at the hem of Europe; in 1986, after years of negotiations, it was finally admitted as a member of the European Community. Now, for the first time in 500 years, it has begun to look to a future within Europe. There are dramatic changes afoot: new roads and infrastructure, new funding, a booming economy, a rush to modernise.

And now, too, there is a growing realisation among travellers that here is a country left untapped for decades, a country of extraordinary diversity, with high mountain peaks and plains of cork trees, rich green valleys and swathes of lushness, 'the garden of Europe,' wrote Coleridge, 'planted by the sea-shore'.

It's the sea you hear about most; the sunny beaches of the Algarve. And how they've been ruined by unrestricted development and mass tourism since the mid-1980s. It's not completely true—you can still find delightful coves without a villa or sunburnt Brit in sight, if you head west of Lagos, east of Faro (or just ten miles inland for rural peace)—but many stretches of this southern seaside have suffered sadly

*The cockerel of Barcelos is the symbol of tourist Portugal, but it's the lively festivals with their folk dances and music that most often charm the visitors. The area around Viana do Castelo is particularly renowned for its brilliant costumes and flower-adorned festivities.*

from being discovered too quickly by too many.

It's not surprising they came here first: the Algarve's Mediterranean climate, protected bays and fishing villages have attracted visitors since the days of the Phoenicians. The Moors were here for some 500 years until finally being uprooted at the end of the thirteenth century —although their name for the area, *Al-Gharb* (meaning, 'the West') remained. The Moors also left a legacy of dark complexions, pretty white chimneys, and groves of oranges, lemons and almonds. Their fondness for sweets has infiltrated the whole nation (try the saccharine bombshell *pudim molotov* for a taste of the richest legacy), and dishes cooked in their unique *cataplana* pressure-cookers are still featured on every Algarve menu.

But what many modern-day visitors to Portugal are also discovering is that there's a good deal more to the country than the sunny Algarve. Even southerners begrudgingly admit that the north, beyond the River Tagus, is the most beautiful part—particularly the provinces of the Minho and the Douro with their densely–wooded hills, terraced vineyards, innumerable small agricultural holdings and old granite villages.

This is the cradle of Portugal, heartland of the Lusitani warrior tribe who, for years, proved a thorn in the ranks of the invading Romans; their name lived on as one of the later Roman provinces, encompassing nearly all of present-day Portugal. Just over a millenium later, in the same area (at Guimaraes), Afonso Henriques was born: the first King of Portugal and the first to fight for Portugal's independence from Spain.

Today, it's the most populated part of the country (although it certainly doesn't strike you as overcrowded—Portugal's total population is only 10 million), with most villagers struggling to make a living out of the difficult soil. Emigration has always been high from here: in the eighteenth century, Brazil was the favoured destination for fortune-seekers; modern-day adventurers have preferred Germany and France.

Remittances from overseas emigrants (an estimated three million Portuguese live abroad) are a welcome support for the economy; and many villages have been transformed by bright new houses, built by returning workers to replace the old family cow-shed-cum-cottage and to stand as a symbol of their freedom from the land. Sometimes the money has run out or the opportunities have dwindled before the last floor has been built—or the worker yields to that uniquely Portuguese sense of nostalgia and yearning called *saudade*, and comes home early —and the half-completed fancy house reverts again to a cow-barn, with pigs in the ornamental fountain, and straw sticking out from the modern painted door.

Emotions run deep in the Portuguese personality. And none are shown off to better effect than the religious passion of the northerners: Catholicism is taken seriously throughout the country, but particularly in the north, where religious festivals, fairs or pilgrimages are a feature of every summer weekend or holy day. They're brilliant, joyous events, with elaborate floral decorations (Vila Franca do Lima's famous *Festas da Senhora das Rosas* features a procession of costumed women bearing huge trays of flowers on their heads), folk dances in local costume, fireworks and bull-running in the streets. Anywhere else in the world, you'd think this was just for tourists. Here in the Minho, it's for real.

Perhaps their days of enjoyment are so passionately celebrated because their lives on the land are so hard. It's rare to see a tractor in these villages: the work is still done by oxen, mule or horses, and even more by hand. It makes a pretty sight— the old wooden carts and hand-carved yokes, the women in their scarves and woollen skirts—but the reality is harsher. Many farmers are looking forward to grants from the European Community which will help them modernise their antiquated methods, which lag far behind those of their EEC neighbours.

Changes are certainly coming—although they're happening faster in the country's three main industrial fields of textiles and clothing, wood and associated products, and china and earthenware. In agriculture (which still occupies some 20 percent of the workforce), there's the difficult nature of the land to contend with: often too steep in the north to allow tractors to work, too dry and poor in the southern Alentejo Plains to eke out more than cork trees, wheat and olives. But gradually, even the vineyard terraces of the Douro Valley are being widened for mechanisation, bringing to an end the days when man alone brought the grape to harvest and port to the Englishman's table.

'The Portuguese and the English have always been the best of friends,' quipped a Captain Frederick Marryat in 1834, 'because we can't get no port wine anywhere else.' True enough, the exceptional conditions under which port grapes are grown and ripened—an extreme 'microclimate' (described as nine months of winter and three months of hell), and a soil of schist which retains the heat of the day—are found nowhere but along the Douro River, in the world's oldest demarcated area, which was established in 1756.

But the Portuguese-English friendship existed long before the English were introduced to port in the late seventeenth century: as far back as 1147, an army of English crusaders, en route for the Holy Land, had helped the Portuguese wrest Lisbon from the Moors. The first of many treaties between the two countries was signed in 1373, and many subsequent marriages cemented the alliance—notably those of Philippa, daughter of John of Gaunt, with Joao I, King of Portugal, in 1386, and of Catherine of Braganca with King Charles II in 1662. Thus two seafaring nations merged—and tea became an English fad, popularised by Catherine.

Ties are still close (most direct foreign investment comes from the UK), although France and West Germany are now the leading trade partners. The people are in fact a fascinating international mix: an influx of nearly a million colonial refugees in the late 1970s (after a radical government granted independence to most remaining overseas territories) provided Portugal with a medley of African races in addition to the older legacy of Moors and Marranos (hereditary Jews whose ancestors were forced to convert during the fifteenth century and who retain some Jewish rituals).

But the Portuguese character has a distinct, shared streak of friendliness. As Lord Caernarvon wrote in 1827, 'Portuguese politeness is delightful, because it is by no means purely artificial, but flows in a great measure from a natural kindness of feeling.' Handshakes are *de rigeur*, kisses on both cheeks common; a warm neighbourliness cossets every town and village. You soon realise why the Portuguese are slow in improving their less-than-efficient telephone system—they obviously much prefer to shout down the street in person, lean out of their windows to conduct a conversation, or stand at their doorways and keep an eye on what's going on. They like to talk, *as palavras sao como as cerejas*, goes a native saying— 'words are like cherries, they get so entangled you can't stop them'.

You can't rush a Portuguese, either. While the boisterous vitality of the many young people (23 percent of the population are under 15) gives a dynamic air to Portuguese society, business lifestyle is rather more sedate. Long lunches are taken very seriously. Enjoying life is taken seriously. And for a Portuguese, there is no better place to enjoy it than on home ground: few Europeans express such passion for their country as do the Portuguese.

Their enthusiasm is infectious: whether you stick to the 500-mile Atlantic

*In the fifteenth century, Portuguese mariners used their sailing expertise to discover the sea-route to India. Today, replicas of their famous caravels, emblazoned with the Cross of the Order of Christ, feature in Viana do Castelo's festival of floral floats. Beja's towering keep (above) harks back to earlier times, when King Dinis filled the land with castles as a defence against Spain.*

17

*The simple pleasures of Portuguese life contrast with an often staggering ornateness in works of art: the ceiling of the* Sala do Imperio *(above) in Évora's* Pousada dos Lóios *is one of the many impressive sights in this former monastery, while the intricately-carved fourteenth century tomb of King Pedro in the Abbey of Alcobaça shows Portuguese sculpture at its most dramatic.*

coastline, venture inland to the northern mountains and southern plains, or travel to the eastern border with Spain, you will discover people of *brandos costumes* or gentle ways—and absurdly picturesque landscapes. There scarcely seems anywhere that isn't pretty—even the never-ending rolling grasslands of the Alentejo have a stark beauty and simplicity, an alluring light drawn from the expanse of sky and golden wheatfields.

But above all, it's the sea that seems to influence Portugal's personality. Hilaire Belloc caught the gist: 'If there is one slice of Christendom, one portion of Europe which was made by the sea more than any other,' he wrote, 'Portugal is that slice, that portion, that belt. Portugal was made by the Atlantic.'

Fishing is still a major industry: even in the trendiest resorts such as Cascais, near Lisbon, you'll find a tenacious fishing community, though their seaside cafés are now called *The John Bull* and *The Wellington*. Just south of Figueira da Foz they use oxen to pull in the nets the traditional way and at Vila do Conde, north of Oporto, the thriving fishing port is complemented by the highly-reputed production of lace—fulfilling the old adage, 'where there are nets there's lace'.

More widespread is the great choice of fish that you find on menus throughout the land, dominated, naturally, by *bacalhau* (salted codfish), the flagship of Portugal's culinary adventures: Portuguese fleets were fishing for cod off the coast of Newfoundland within a few years of America's discovery, and the fishermen's method of salting and drying the cod to preserve it on the journey home created something of a national obsession: supplies now have to come from Norway to meet the demand, and cookbooks always like to tell you that there are 365 different ways to cook it, one for every day of the year.

Fortunately, there are other choices in the fish repertoire—not only the equally famous grilled sardines, but also squid, trout and sole, seafood paella and even eel stew. The Portuguese love their fish—both catching it and eating it. Some of the most impressive fishermen are those poised high on the rocks at the westernmost headland of Europe—Cape St Vincent, near Sagres—where they drop their lines hundreds of feet straight down into the crashing waves below.

Sagres is a sea-mark of psychological importance to the Portuguese for it was here that Prince Henry the Navigator (one of the youngest, most serious sons of Philippa and Joao I) established his School of Navigation, and built the first caravels in which his explorers were to venture round the coast of Africa, creeping ever closer to India.

The fascination with the sea lingers on, much as if Portugal were an island. Even inland, reservoirs hold a strong appeal, and the popularity of the country's 19 spas has as much to do, perhaps, with the mystique of water as with the belief in its medical benefits. The mountains where most of the spas are located do not hold the same allure for the Portuguese; they remain wild and unexplored, hiding incredibly remote villages —like Soajo with its famous granite granaries, tucked high among the mountains of Geres and Peneda, or the tiny community of Piodao, on the edge of Serra da Estrela, its houses all of shale and its nights quieter than any you will have ever known.

These are the places which make Portugal special: the villages on the rough edge of nature, set apart, tough and independent, either walled as a fortress like the lovely Obidos, or carved into, and out of the rock like the extraordinary wild Monsanto.

These, and their opposite—the exuberant rich architecture of the sixteenth century Manueline style, laden with gold from Brazil; the fabulous *azulejo* tilework in almost every major church; the silk brocade vestments and golden chalices in almost every museum give the country a range of many notes. Even Lisbon—most of whose monuments were devastated in 1755 by a massive earthquake—has an unexpected element of rural life, in the medieval backstreets of the Alfama, where the soul-searing *fado* music is said to have originated, and where residents still proudly maintain a separate sense of identity.

Built, like Rome, on seven hills, and commanding the Tagus Estuary, Lisbon has been the capital of the country since 1385. The city's magnificent appearance from the river,'What beauties doth Lisboa first unfold! Her image floating on that noble tide,' wrote Byron, has always won her critics over (it was one of the few nice things Byron wrote about the country). But you'd hardly call Lisbon as a whole magnificent: with its old-fashioned cable cars, art nouveau cafés, shabby nineteenth century houses and mosaic pavements, its appeal today is as much the air of faded glory as the new dash of entrepreneurship.

The attractions are a bizarre mix, reflecting the city's own diverse character: the stunning gilded chapels of the Churches of Sao Roque and Madre de Deus reveal all the artistic wealth of Portugal's Golden Age, the *fado* confirms its passion and poignancy. All the views of the city (and there are many) have a dreamy quality.

Oporto, the country's second city (seen with Oporto eyes, unquestionably the first) seems very much more brisk and businesslike: this is the heart of the country's most important economic area and you can feel the pulse, not only in the city itself but also in Vila Nova de Gaia, on the other side of the River Douro, where all the port wine houses have their cellars.

Like Lisbon, Oporto has its faded, shabby side, too, although it's full of atmosphere: narrow streets in the Ribeira district climb up in a tangle from the river, flapping with laundry, smelling of fish. Elsewhere, but in the rumbunctious Bolhao Market most of all, Oporto people seem to love the buzz of being busy: a teasing Portuguese saying claims 'Coimbra (the university city, famous for its brand of *fado*) sings, Braga (famous for its churches) prays, Lisbon shows off and Oporto works.'

But in this aggressive new era of sink or swim, all of Portugal is having to learn to work. Quaint, money-hungry delights such as the narrow-gauge railways of the north have been axed (much to the horror of tourists and tourism officials). A new emphasis on international links is taking precedence—bridges, motorways and high-speed railway services to Spain mark the first, most symbolic overland links with Europe that Portugal has ever had.

It will be a new experience for Portugal to go inland. Many of its unique attractions will undoubtedly be sacrificed in the process. But the country should also become stronger. With its traditional penchant for trade, it will find its own niche in the new Europe, and perhaps make a surprising discovery en route: an unfamiliar sense of belonging, a sense of coming in from the edge.

*Portugal has always had a close affinity with the sea. Along its 837 km (520 miles) of Atlantic coastline are long-established fishing communities, with a tradition in brightly coloured craft: in Aveiro (top, centre), the flat-bottomed barcos moliçeiros that are used to collect seaweed from the estuary are decorated like a pack of cards. At nearby Praia de Mira (above), where net-mending is a daily chore, oxen are still used to haul in the nets.*

*One of the most extraordinary places in Portugal, Monsanto (right) is literally carved out of a granite hill, 760m (2,500 ft) high. First colonised by the Lusitanian tribe, it claims to be the oldest settlement in the country; the dwellings seem almost prehistoric, camouflaged among rocks, unlike their sunny counterparts further south (top) near Portalegre.*

For centuries beloved by poets, royalty and the British, Sintra still wooes visitors with its verdant mystique. The town is dominated by the conical chimneys of the National Palace (left) which dates back to the thirteenth century and still hosts foreign dignitaries. But for eccentricity, nothing can beat the Disneyland concoction of the hilltop Pena Palace (far left), built by King Ferdinande in 1840 in a crazy assortment of neo-Gothic, neo-Manueline, Moorish and Baroque styles. The interior—equally whimsical—has scarcely changed since the royal family last resided here in 1910.

The Portuguese have an eye for colour and a talent for tidiness: even the humblest home uses bright, glazed tiles, paintwork or lace to their best effects.

The elegant little seaside town of Costa Nova, just south of Aveiro, sports a unique line in striped houses—a convenient visual distraction for when the Atlantic winds make the sea too dangerous for swimming.

The Convento de Cristo at Tomar, once the headquarters of the military-
monastic Order of Christ (originally the 'Order of the Knights Templar'), is a
formidable artistic display of the Order's power and prestige. Its elaborate
Manueline nave is almost hidden by the Renaissance-style cloisters. But the
highlight is the nave's chapter-house window (right), which encapsulates all the
nautical themes of the fifteenth century Age of Discovery in a Manueline tangle
of carved coral, seaweed, globes and ropes. It was during this time that Prince
Henry the Navigator (statue below) was the Order's Governor; he used its
emblem, the red Cross of Christ, on the sails of his discoverers' ships.

Infante D. Henrique
MCDIX MCMLX

The three greatest monuments in the land: the fourteenth century Batalha Abbey (far left), a masterpiece of Portuguese Gothic and Manueline art; the immense twelfth century Alcobaça Abbey (left), which once housed 999 monks; and the grandiose eighteenth century Mafra Palace Monastery (below) which has 5,200 doorways, 2,500 windows and a Rococo library for 35,000 books.

*Coiled high above the Mondego River, Coimbra (once the capital of Portugal) is the home of the country's oldest university, founded in 1290. The university's main courtyard (below) is flanked by sixteenth century buildings and dominated by a Baroque clock-tower nicknamed* A Cabra—*the goat.*

Coimbra University's most
sumptuous building is the Baroque
Library, an extravagant gift from King
João V whose portrait (below) gazes
out on gilded carved woodwork,
lacquered Chinoiserie, and tables of
ebony, rosewood and jacaranda.
Today's students read their books
elsewhere.

*Aveiro (opposite) is one of the most delightful towns on the Costa da Prata, laced with canals that lead out into a large, shallow estuary (the Ria). A thriving port throughout the Middle Ages, Aveiro's fortunes faltered when the River Vouga silted up in the 1570s, isolating it from the sea. A canal was finally cut through in 1808, and prosperity was restored. Low-slung, high-prowed moliceiro boats, used for collecting seaweed for fertiliser, are unique to this area. At nearby Praia de Mira (left), the boats follow an ancient Phoenician design, unlike those of the Algarve (top, left).*

Along the Algarve, west of Faro, rocky coves and crannies provide the perfect shelter for sunbathers. Fishermen keep a beach for themselves at Albufeira (far right), which is the most popular resort on the coast, while at Olhão, (top, right) east of Faro, tourism has hardly touched the traditional way of life.

*Religious processions and ceremonies, such as these in Lagoa and Silves (left, and below) are an important part of Easter celebrations. In the Costa Verde region (far right), appearances are taken seriously in every festival; and at Alte's annual Folk Fair, both man and beast turn out in their Sunday best.*

One of the Algarve's greatest artistic
treasures is the Church of São
Lourenço in Almansil (above), its
walls covered with magnificent
eighteenth century azulejos. The art
of making glazed and painted tiles
was originally introduced to Portugal
by the Moors; by the seventeenth
century an azulejo craze began to
sweep the country, with
multicoloured and blue-and-white
azulejos filling churches, public
buildings, parks and palaces: the late
eighteenth century Estói Palace near
Faro shows a typical fondness for
mythological and bucolic rural scenes
(right).

(Following page)
*In Belém, a few miles west of Lisbon's city centre, beats the pulse of national pride: it was from here in 1497 that Vasco da Gama set sail for India, fulfilling years of exploration around the coast of Africa initiated by Prince Henry the Navigator. In 1960, a vast Monument to the Discoveries was erected in Belém to commemorate the 500th anniversary of Henry's death. Resembling the prow of a ship, it features Henry, Luís de Camões (who wrote a famous epic poem on the voyage) and other heroes of the time.*

The Moors occupied the Algarve for
nearly 500 years and left a legacy of
Arabic language and cuisine, bright
white houses and lovely minarets of
chimneys like the one above.
Voluptuous fountains (right) are part
of the Baroque fantasy of Estói Palace,
near Faro.

The old quarter of Portugal's second city, Oporto (above), tumbles down from the Cathedral and Bishop's Palace to the River Douro below. In 1415, Oporto's most famous son, Prince Henry the Navigator (statue, left), took command of a fleet of warships here which took part in capturing Ceuta from the Moors. The locals were so enthusiastic in supplying the squadron with all their meat supplies that they were left only with offal—hence earning their nickname, tripeiros, tripe-eaters. Even today, tripe is an Oporto specialty.

Bullfights in Portugal are not as
common or as gruesome as in Spain
(the bull isn't killed in the arena) but
they're just as spectacular: a mounted
toureiro in eighteenth-century style
costume first engages the bull in a
dramatic display of riding prowess,
avoiding the animal's charges while
attempting to plant darts in its back.
An eight-man team then tries to
grapple the beast to the ground, with
the most suicidally-minded literally
throwing themselves between the
animal's horns.

Mist shrouds one of Oporto's three bridges across the River Douro—the two-tiered *Ponte de Dom Luís I* (top left)—which connects the city with Vila Nova de Gaia, home of port wine lodges such as Sandeman's. *Before the era of rail and road transport, the wine was brought down from the Upper Douro in square-sailed* barcos rabelos: *the only ones left now are those moored outside the lodges (centre left) for advertising purposes.*

Like a jilted bride—all frills and no admirer—the glittering 'Arab Hall' ballroom is the incongruous pride and joy of 0porto's nineteenth century Stock Exchange building. An imitation of the Alhambra's Moorish style, it took 18 years and 18 kilos (40 pounds) of gold to create.

Built on seven hills beside the River Tagus, Lisbon is a narcissistic city, indulging in panoramas: from the ancient Castle of São Jorge (left), the view stretches west to the April 25 Bridge, while from Belém (below, left), the silhouette of the Monument to the Discoveries *frames the dawn.* On the street, pomp and charm are Lisbon's qualities: the eighteenth century triumphal arch and bronze equestrian statue of King José I in the riverfront Praça do Comércio (below) contrast with the simple brightness of a Belém residential district.

The monastery of Jerónimos (above) in Belém is the most thrilling example of Portugal's unique style of Manueline art, remarkable for its detailed carving and magnificent vaulting. It was founded by King Manuel in 1502 soon after the successful sea voyage of Vasco da Gama from Belém to India—an exploit subsequently commemorated in literature, architecture and azulejo panels (left and right) although religious (and not-so-religious) themes remained the most popular azulejo subjects.

*Lisbon's Coach Museum in Belém (below) houses one of the largest collections of gilded carriages in the world. Dating from the sixteenth century, they feature painted and padded interiors, statues and ornate mouldings. Simpler sights catch the eye in the backstreets of Alfama (right) or among the ancient mansions of Viana do Castelo (far right).*

Agriculture involves 20 percent of the Portuguese workforce, but methods are laborious and archaic: in the north, oxen and mules still outnumber tractors, and life in villages such as this one (left) near Arcos de Valdevez is often hard. Grants from the European Community are now slowly helping to modernise many farms and lifestyles, but things are unlikely to change very fast for the small population of gypsies (right) who still travel the byways of the Alentejan Plains.

On 13 May 1917, and on the 13th of the following five months, an apparition of the Virgin Mary appeared to three peasant girls in Fátima. The town is now one of the most important places of pilgrimage in the Catholic world, attracting a constant stream of devotees throughout the year, and up to 100,000 pilgrims on the anniversaries of the Virgin's appearance. Many cross the huge esplanade leading to the Basilica (right) on their knees.

RECONCILIAI-VOS COM DE

*Monuments span every age: a Roman bridge (right) crosses the lovely Lima River at Ponte de Lima in the Minho province; the modern neo-Byzantine Church of Santa Luzia (below) looks down on Viana do Castelo from its Monte Luzia summit; and from the twelfth century comes one of the most curious buildings in Portugal, the Charola (bottom), the 16-sided temple of Tomar's Convento de Cristo. The Knights Templar are said to have attended mass here on horseback.*

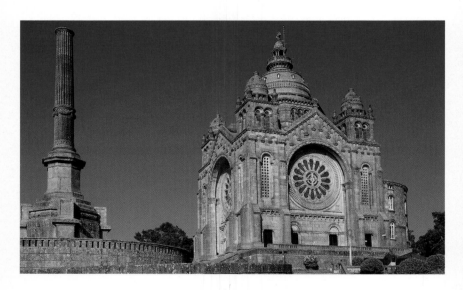

The discovery of gold and diamonds in Portugal's colony of Brazil led to an outburst of architectural indulgences during the seventeenth and eighteenth centuries. The delightful Royal Palace of Queluz (above), built between 1758-94, and inspired by Versailles, is the finest Rococo showpiece in the land. Queen Maria I spent her last mad years here in the early 1800s, wandering in the formal gardens of box hedges and statuary, topiary and fountains. The neo-classical church of Bom Jesus do Monte (right) followed the eighteenth century trend for elaborately decorated facades but created a new spectacle by standing at the top of a monumental, ziz-zagging Baroque staircase.

In Évora, one of Portugal's most gracious towns, a second century Roman temple (above) overlooks the Church of the Lóios, built on the site of a Moorish castle. The nearby cathedral, its portal flanked by bearded apostles (left) was built where the Moors once had their mosque. A statue of Queen Saint Isabel (top, left) keeps watch on her former palace in Estremoz, now a luxurious pousada with its own thirteenth century keep.

Outdoor markets are more than just a place for fruit and vegetables: in the vast Thursday market at Barcelos (above) all kinds of produce are for sale, from pottery to pigeons, carved yokes to souvenir cockerels, roast chestnuts to cheese, lace to live rabbits. Caldas da Rainha (top, right) hosts a smaller, but equally lively market every Saturday.

*Blue and white are Portugal's dominant colours, most noticeably on buildings, such as this clock-tower (left) in Coruche, and in azulejo panels (below). Polychrome azulejos were a Rococo favourite in palaces and mansions, but today even bullfight stadiums (bottom) enjoy multicoloured designs.*

*(Above) Conimbriga, near Coimbra, is the largest Roman site in Portugal and the most impressive legacy of their 600-year rule. Once a major town on the Braccaraia (Braga) to Olissipo (Lisbon) road, Conimbriga fell to the Suebi tribe in AD468 and was deserted in favour of Coimbra. Among the many well-preserved mosaics is this one (above) of Perseus, offering Medusa's head to a sea-monster.*

For the Romans, the Lima River (above) was too lovely to be true: believing it to be the River of Forgetfulness they refused to cross until their commander had seized the standard and plunged in, shouting the names of his legionaries from the other side. At Constância (left) the poet Luís de Camões took refuge for three years after an injudicious love affair at court. Perhaps he would have been safer in the far northeast corner of Trás-os-Montes—'the province beyond the mountains'—where the ancient walled citadel of Bragança (top, left) has stood remote and isolated for nearly 900 years.

# AN A TO Z OF FACTS AND FIGURES

## A

**Australia** Many Portuguese are convinced that an expedition in 1511 by António de Abren and Francisco Serrão discovered Australia 200 years before Captain Cook. Hard evidence is lacking but in 1847 a bunch of ancient keys were discovered on the shore of Corio Bay near Melbourne, and the remains of a very old shipwreck were sighted in 1836 at Warrnambol near Geelong. Further evidence includes a chiselled carving of a head, discovered in 1838 by the English explorer George Grey—the aborigines didn't possess chisels at that time!

**Azores** The nine-island archipelago of the Azores lie 1,440 km (895 miles) west of Lisbon. They were originally discovered by the Portuguese in 1427 and colonised soon after.

**Azulejos** Blue-and-white or polychrome glazed wall tiles appear everywhere in Portugal. The *azulejo* craze began to sweep the country in the early seventeenth century after the art was introduced by the Moors. At first a variety of colours, the tiles became predominantly blue and white under the influence of Chinese Ming dynasty porcelain imported into Europe. Some of the most impresive *azulejo* panels date from the eighteenth century and depict religious scenes, as in Almancil's São Lourenço Church, Évora's Lójos Church and Barcelos' Church of NS do Terço. See Lisbon's Tile Museum, in the Convent of Madre de Deus, for an excellent display on the development of *azulejo* styles.

## B

**Bacalhau** The Portuguese began fishing for cod off Newfoundland soon after America was discovered, drying and salting the fish to make it last the journey home. They've been passionate about salted codfish ever since, concocting 365 different ways to cook it.

**Bullfights** The big difference between Spanish and Portuguese bullfighting is that in Portugal the bull is not killed in the ring. Indeed, it's a much more refined affair altogether, with mounted horsemen (wearing magnificent eighteenth century-style costumes) inciting the bull to charge until it is exhausted.

## C

**Caldo Verde** A regular menu item, this jade-green cabbage soup is the country's most famous dinnertime treat. It actually tastes much better than it sounds, and often includes slices of smoked sausage.

**Citanias** Celtic fortified hilltop settlements are scattered throughout the north, but the one at Briteiros, near Braga, is probably the best preserved. Believed to have been the last stronghold against the Romans, it features the foundations of over 150 huts.

**Cockerels** The ubiquitous gaudy symbol of tourist Portugal traces its origins to Barcelos: a legend from here recounts how a fourteenth century Galician pilgrim was saved from the gallows when he successfully bet that a roasted cock on the judge's table would stand up and crow to proclaim his innocence. The famous market at Barcelos sells hundreds of the things—live, roasted and fired into ghastly pottery souvenirs.

## D

**Dom Dinis** If you wonder who built all the castles you see in Portugal, chances are it was Dom (King) Dinis, who ruled from 1279 to 1325, strengthening Portugal's defences with a castle-building frenzy. Romantics should head for the one at Almourol, set in its own island in the Tagus River.

**Douro Valley** This beautiful northern region is famous for its vineyards which climb up steep terraces on either side of the broad Douro River. In 1756 the Upper Douro became the world's first wine-producing area to be demarcated.

## E

**Earthquake** On All Saints' Day in 1755 Lisbon was devastated by a massive earthquake. Fires and tidal waves followed, killing 40,000 citizens and destroying most of the city's finest monuments.

# F

**Festivals** There's nothing like a Portuguese *festa* to give you a feel for the place: celebrated with enormous enthusiasm, especially in the north, they invariably feature traditional folksongs and dancing in local costume, elaborate floral decorations and fireworks.

**Fado** Reflecting the Latin origins of its name—*fatum*, meaning destiny—*fado* is a sad, lyrical lament which first became popular in Lisbon's Alfama district in the 1830s. Coimbra has a more intellectual version.

# G

**Golf** The Algarve boasts some of Europe's best golf-courses, such as the 27 hole championship Vale do Lobo course near Faro. Golf has been played in Portugal since 1890 when the Oporto Golf Club became the second course on the Continent.

**Guimaraes** This ancient northern town was the birthplace of Afonso Henriques, the first King of Portugal, who finally won recognition from the Pope for his new Christian kingdom in 1179.

Modern-day fans know it for its football team.

# H

**Henry the Navigator** The serious young son of Joao I and his English queen, Philippa, Prince Henry was the catalyst for the extraordinary fifteenth century Age of Discoveries: he established a School of Navigation at Sagres and sent his mariners ever further round the coast of Africa to find the sea route to India (he himself never went further than Tangier). He died in 1460, 38 years before the goal was reached.

# I

**Ines de Castro** The Spanish lover of Prince Dom Pedro is more famous for what happened in her death than in her life: believing her family to be a threat, Pedro's father, Dom Afonso V, sanctioned her murder in 1355. Two years later, when Dom Pedro took the throne, he had her body exhumed and crowned, and compelled the nobility to kiss her decomposed hand. (He's also said to have eaten the hearts of her murderers!)

**Inquisition** Yes, Portugal had its Inquisition horrors, too, although they generally weren't as bloodthirsty as those of Spain. The Inquisition's headquarters was established in 1537 where Lisbon's National Theatre now

stands. The persecutions only ended in the latter half of the eighteenth century.

# J

**Jews** Portugal has a strong Jewish heritage which dates back to the time of the Moors. The largest influx arrived in 1492 when Spain expelled their Jews: many settled in places like Braganca, Guarda and Belmonte, contributing greatly to the silk industry.

# K

**Knights Templar** The Order of the Knights Templar was founded in AD1118 during the First Crusade to guard the pilgrim routes to the Holy Land and help fight the Moors. Transformed into the Order of Christ in the fourteenth century, its red Cross of Christ became the emblem of the Age of Discoveries.

# L

**Luis de Camoes** Perhaps the most celebrated Portuguese literary figure, Camoes is the poet of the Great Discoveries: his epic *The Lusiads* (1572) recounts the voyage of Vasco da Gama to India.

**Lusitanians** The fierce Lusitanian tribe of central Portugal kept the Romans at bay for years.

The name lived on as one of the later Roman provinces.

**Madeira**  One of the oldest quality wines of all, Madeira has a unique taste because of the island's volcanic soil and the gradual heating method used during fermentation (called *estafas*). Madeira is blended, matured and fortified and lives longer than any other wine in the world.

**Manueline**  Portugal's most impressive style of architecture, which flowered in the sixteenth century reign of Manuel I, reflects the excitement of the Age of Discoveries in exuberant maritime motifs, armillary spheres and triumphal arches. See the Jeronimos Monastery at Belem for the Manueline style at its finest.

**Miradouro**  Almost every Portuguese town has its own *miradouro*—a viewpoint or belvedere, often surrounded with a garden. Lisbon, a narcissistic city, has 17 of them.

**N**

**Nicolau Nasoni**  An eighteenth century architect of Italian origin, Nasoni is most famous for his whimsical Baroque creation, the *Solar de Mateus* (whose romantic picture adorns every Mateus Rosé wine bottle).

**Obidos**  One of the prettiest walled towns in the country, Obidos has charmed visitors for centuries: in 1228 the young Queen Isabella liked it so much that King Dinis gave it to her as a gift, establishing a custom that lasted until 1833.

**P**

**Pig**  Pig is king when it comes to favourite meat dishes in Portugal: garlicky sausages, smoked ham, and suckling pig are just some of the specialities. Prehistoric granite pigs remain a mystery of the northeast Tras-os-Montes region.

**Pillory**  The *pelourinho* stone column is a feature of almost every town and village, and often beautifully carved. Criminals were once tied to the pillory's metal hooks.

**Port**  'The Portuguese and the English have always been the best of friends,' quipped a Captain Frederick Marryat in 1834, 'because we can't get no Port Wine anywhere else.' True enough: the country's most famous beverage is made only with grapes grown in the Douro Valley, where conditions are perfect. It is fortified by the addition of grape brandy and matured in casks or large oak vats, traditionally at Vila Nova de Gaia, opposite Oporto. The wine can be red or white (there's nothing better than chilled white port with grilled sardines) but it's the red, or ruby port, that most people know and love. The best places to sample port are at the Port Wine Institutes in Lisbon and Oporto or the port lodges in Vila Nova de Gaia.

**Pousada**  The 30 government-owned *pousadas* are small, luxury hotels in places of outstanding historic interest or scenic beauty. Monks and kings will feel at home—many *pousadas* are in converted monasteries, convents or castles.

**Q**

**Queluz**  The Royal Palace of Queluz, near Lisbon, is a blancmange-pink Rococo fantasy inspired by Versailles. Visiting heads of state get the privilege of staying here.

**Queijo de Serra**  Portugal's best (and most expensive) cheese is made from pure ewes' milk in the mountainous Serra da Estrela region.

**R**

**Revolution**  The unpopularity of a repressive government and of drawn-out wars in the African colonies finally led to a bloodless coup on 25 April, 1974. The Revolution brought dramatic changes: independence to the African colonies, nationalisation, and massive land seizures in the Alentejo. A new democratic constitution was drawn up in 1976.

**Rio de Onor** Two tiny villages with this same name are on either side of the northern Spanish-Portuguese border: a chain across a path marks the frontier, but the villagers take no notice. They speak a curious dialect of both languages.

**Saudade** An untranslatable, uniquely Portuguese emotion, meaning something like nostalgia or yearning, and best expressed in the laments of *fado*.

**Sintra** 'Perhaps the most delightful (village) in Europe,' wrote Byron, 'a glorious Eden'. The magical forested hills of Sintra, 28 km (15 miles) northwest of Lisbon, have long attracted visitors: for six centuries it was the favourite summer residence of the Kings of Portugal.

**Tagus River** A convenient geographic dividing line between the mountains of the north and the plateaux and plains of the south. Lisbon commands the Tagus Estuary but the source lies in Spain. As rivers go, it's rather boring.

**Trams** If you do nothing else in Lisbon, you must take one of the city's funky old trams that wheeze and clang up the steepest streets—Number 28 is the best. In Oporto (fewer options), try the Number 1 to the seaside.

**Ucanha** At the bottom of a quiet, cosy lane, this tiny village near Lamego hides a surprise: a huge fourteenth century fortified bridge.

**Vinho Verde** Literally 'green wine', a young brew from the green province of the Minho. Vinho verde is slightly effervescent and best drunk chilled (stick to the whites—the reds taste rather odd!).

**Vasco da Gama** Portugal's most famous mariner, da Gama discovered the sea route to India in 1498, returning to Lisbon the following year with the first of the spices that would enrich the country.

**Wine of the Dead** The locals of Boticas village (near Chaves) first buried their bottles of wine to hide them from invading French troops in 1809. It tasted so good afterwards they continued the

practice and nicknamed it *Wine of the Dead*. You can try a glass of this surprisingly lively brew at the village *Café de Armindo*.

**Youth Hostels** Two of the most atmospheric (and spartan) youth hostels in Portugal can be found at opposite ends of the country: one is situated inside the fort at Sagres (where Henry the Navigator had his School of Navigation), and the other high in the Geres mountains, three kilometres above the granite village of Lindoso.

**Z** _____

**Zambujeiro Dolmen** Not far from Evora, amidst fields of wild flowers and cork trees, lies the largest dolmen in the Iberian Peninsula, some five metres (17 ft) high and 5,000 years old, it's a very strange stone indeed.

# INDEX